CUTTY SARK

A SOUVENIR GUIDE TO THE STORY OF THE LAST OF THE TEA CLIPPERS

CUTTY SARK

GREENWICH

In Appreciation

The Cutty Sark Trust is indebted to those members of the public who contributed to the preservation of this much loved national treasure. We have also had very generous support from the Heritage Lottery Fund, the Department of Culture, Media and Sport, Greenwich Council, the Sammy Ofer Foundation, Michael Edwards, the Stavros Niarchos Foundation, the London Development Agency and Berry Brothers and Rudd which made the Conservation Project 2006-2012 possible.

Published by: The Cutty Sark Trust.
Copyright: The Cutty Sark Trust.

Supported by
The National Lottery®
through the Heritage Lottery Fund

heritage
lottery fund

FOREWORD ⤸

It is sometimes overlooked that, as well as the palaces, castles, cathedrals, churches and houses that make up the historic landscape of the United Kingdom, we are even more fortunate that a significant number of ships and boats have also survived. As a group they reflect much of the great maritime history of Britain as a nation, from Henry VIII's *Mary Rose* and Nelson's *Victory*, Brunel's revolutionary *Great Britain*, and indeed to the 'little ships of Dunkirk.'

Among these vessels, probably none have as many sea miles as *Cutty Sark*. But she owes her very special place, not because of her tea cargoes or her record-breaking runs home from Australia. It is because she is the very epitome of sail. When we imagine a sailing ship in all her glory, it is the image of the elegant clipper that is most likely to be conjured up. And no clipper ship was finer, faster or more famous than *Cutty Sark*.

Yet her survival into the twentieth century, let alone the twenty-first, was never certain, especially following the fire of 2007. Her presence in Greenwich today is due to the determination of a number of individuals, in particular His Royal Highness The Duke of Edinburgh, together with wonderful financial support from institutions, from charitable foundations and from many members of the public, who have ensured that this most beautiful of ships would be saved for future generations to enjoy.

We welcome you on board.

Lord Sterling of Plaistow
Chairman, The Cutty Sark Trust

CONTENTS

Right: Cutty Sark's figurehead Nannie.

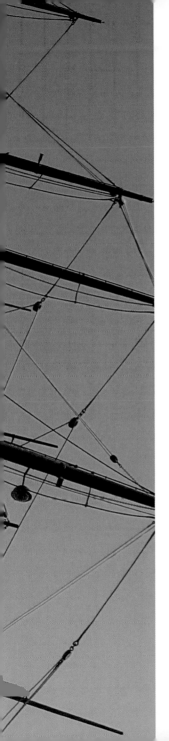

INTRODUCTION ✒

It is amazing that *Cutty Sark* has survived.

Many of the clipper ships that sailed the China Seas with her in the second half of the nineteenth century were wrecked, foundered or were lost in their first few years. Not many lasted more than twenty years. Only seven saw the twentieth century. By the mid-1920s *Cutty Sark* was the only one still afloat.

She does not owe her longevity to an uneventful career. She lost masts in storms and hurricanes, had rudders ripped off by high seas and collided with other ships.

In voyages to almost every major port in the world, carrying everything from tea of the highest quality to shark 'bones', men were washed overboard; at least one killing took place on board and a captain committed suicide. In danger of falling apart from neglect, she was saved and retired from the sea, but she still came close to almost certain destruction on another five occasions.

She is now safely berthed in the Royal Borough of Greenwich, chosen for preservation as a memorial both to the great days of sail and to all those who served in the merchant service. One of the nation's greatest maritime treasures, *Cutty Sark* is a major attraction in Maritime Greenwich, a World Heritage Site. This is particularly appropriate as her fame spreads far beyond Britain – she is one of the most famous vessels in the world. This is not just because of her history, or even just because of what she represents. It is also because she is the most beautiful of all sailing ships.

An early 19th-century Chinese screen, showing all the phases of tea production, packing and transport.

THE CHINA TEA TRADE

C*utty Sark* was built for one purpose – to bring tea back from China to London quickly. Tea, produced exclusively in China until the mid-nineteenth century, had been introduced to Europe by the Portuguese and Dutch. It reached England in the late 1650s, and was made fashionable among the aristocracy by the Portuguese princess Catherine of Braganza, who married Charles II in 1662.

Despite being heavily taxed, tea quickly became popular among all social classes, thanks to an enormous smuggling industry. More 'illegal' tea came into Britain through the Netherlands than through the legal importers, the East India Company. In 1784, determined to support the Company's monopoly on tea, the British Government slashed the duty levied on it from 112 per cent to 12 ½ per cent. Suddenly tea was relatively inexpensive and it moved from being one of life's luxuries to one of its necessities. The Temperance Movement, which was particularly active in the 1840s and 50s, gave it a further boost by promoting tea as an alternative to alcohol. Tea imports boomed.

The East India Company had to pay the Chinese for tea (and silk) with silver, as there were very few Western-produced goods the Chinese wanted to buy. To redress this trade 'imbalance', the Company grew opium in India and sold it to smugglers to run into China. There, of course, it was paid for in silver. Opium had been banned by the Chinese authorities in 1799, but they could not halt the traffic. When, in 1839, the Chinese authorities seized and destroyed shipments of opium in Canton (Guangdong), this was taken as an affront to free trade and Britain declared war. No match for the British navy, the Chinese were forced to cede Hong Kong, and open up a number of their ports to trade, including Shanghai and Fuzhou.

TEA.
THEA SINENSIS.

A second war between 1856 and 1860 resulted in even more ports being opened up to Europeans, including the important tea port of Hankou, hundreds of miles up the Yangtze River.

Ironically, the East India Company saw little direct benefit, since in 1834 the free-trade movement forced the government to end the Company's monopoly with China. For ship-owners, however, with demand for tea rocketing, there were fortunes to be made.

Left: Camellia sinensis - tea plant.

Right: Catherine of Braganza, Portuguese wife of Charles II, who made tea fashionable in Britain. By or after Dirk Stoop, circa 1660-1661.

The tea clipper 'Thermopylae', by F.I. Sorensen. Launched in 1868, *Thermopylae* was one of the most successful tea clippers.

THE RISE OF THE CLIPPERS ⌒

The term 'clipper' came into use in the USA in the early nineteenth century, specifically describing the small schooners and brigs of Chesapeake Bay which had eluded the British navy during the War of 1812. It simply meant a fast vessel – one which could 'go at a clip'. It was not until the 1830s that the qualities of these craft were scaled-up into larger vessels. Shipbuilders began to re-think some of the assumptions about ship design and a number of ships were built which made very fast passages from China to New York. Then, in 1849, came the discovery of gold in California. This led to a huge boom in shipbuilding – and a demand for large, fast vessels, capable of tackling the awesome seas around Cape Horn.

British shipbuilders may have been inspired by the American examples, which began bringing tea to London in 1850, but they did not directly copy them. In Aberdeen, Alexander Hall & Sons had developed their own prototype for a new style of ship, and they would go on to become the most prolific builder of clippers. The characteristic of this new type of vessel was a long narrow hull, a sharp bow, a yacht-like appearance, raking masts and a very, very large sail area.

The design created not only a fast ship but also, for the British, a tax-efficient one. Traditionally, ships were assessed for duties by taking the length and multiplying it by a notional percentage for depth, which was not related to a vessel's actual depth. This of course resulted in deep ships, which had a good carrying capacity but were slow sailers. But in 1854 the rules changed – duty was now to be calculated by a formula including the area of the hull at three cross-sections. The clipper's long narrow hull and sharp bow meant a very small area at the forward point of measurement, so its owner paid less duty than for a ship built to traditional design.

British vessels tended to be smaller than their American counterparts. However, their hulls were planked with hardwoods from Britain's colonies, not soft pine, so they were less prone to damage. And American competition in the tea trade did not last for long: in 1857 the USA slid into a deep recession, leaving a huge amount of surplus shipping. The British ship-owners were left to compete for trade supremacy largely among themselves.

GREAT RACE

OF THE

TEA SHIPS,

WITH THE FIRST

NEW SEASON'S TEAS.

PRICE OF TEAS REDUCED.

THE "Taeping," "Ariel," "Fiery Cross," and "Serica" have arrived, with others in close pursuit, with something like **FORTY-FIVE MILLION POUNDS OF NEW TEA** on board—half a year's consumption for the **United Kingdom.** This enormous weight coming suddenly into the London Docks, Shippers are compelled to submit to **MUCH LOWER PRICES,** in order to make sales.

We are thus enabled to make a Reduction of FOURPENCE in the pound.

4/0 down to - - 3/8
3/8   „   - - 3/4
3/4   „   - - 3/0

And so on downwards.

We may add the above Ships have brought a few lots of must unusual fine quality.

Reduction takes place on Friday the 21st inst.

135, OXFORD STREET;
57, STRETFORD ROAD; and
171, STRETFORD ROAD—
    "Great Northern."

BURGON & CO.,

TEA MERCHANTS.

THE TEA RACES

F or more than 150 years, the British had been content to buy tea with little concern about how long it had taken to reach them. Tea, after all, is a dry product with a shelf-life of three years or so. Suddenly, however, tea that had taken only three- and-a-half months to arrive was available. The Victorians, with their relish for novelty, began to demand not just 'fresh' tea but particularly the very first of a season's tea to arrive (very like the competition that began a hundred years later to drink the first bottles of Beaujolais Nouveau).

To secure the valuable first shipment, which could be sold at the highest price, tea merchants gave incentives to the ship-owners. From 1861 they also offered an additional premium of ten shillings per ton on the first tea delivered to London.

Competition among ships intensified and the legendary tea clipper races began. Of these, none was closer than the race of 1866. In May that year, five British ships left Fuzhou within hours of each other. Ninety-nine days and 15,000 miles later, *Ariel* reached the Kent coast ten minutes ahead of *Taeping*. But *Taeping* found a tug more quickly and snatched the lead. The crew on board *Ariel* may have still felt that they could win – she was making for the East India Docks while *Taeping* was heading further up the Thames to the London Docks. But *Ariel* was a little deeper in draft than *Taeping* and had a frustrating wait for the tide to rise before she could enter the Docks. As a result, *Taeping* managed to unload her cargo ahead of *Ariel* and was the winner by just twenty minutes.

The owners of the two ships realised that their cargoes, and those of the three ships which would be arriving shortly, would flood the London market. They feared that the merchants would use any dispute about the result of the race as an excuse not to pay the premium. So they secretly agreed not to argue about whether the race was to the Thames or to the dock or to the quayside, but instead to split the bonus. However, never again was the ten shilling premium offered. But nothing could stop the rivalry among the ships to make the season's fastest passage.

Left: Poster advertising tea from the great clipper race of 1866.

The Great China Race: The Clipper Ships 'Taeping' and 'Ariel' passing the Lizard 6 September 1866 on their homeward voyage from Foo-Chow-Foo, by Thomas Goldsworth Dutton, 1866.

John Willis and his new ship

C*utty Sark* was commissioned by John Willis, a Scotsman based in London, who had been a ship's master himself at nineteen, bringing his first tea cargo home in 1846. Seven years later he retired from the sea to concentrate on running the shipping business his father had established.

John Willis had used a number of shipbuilders to create his fleet, but for the new ship which would become *Cutty Sark* he went to a company which had only been established for a year – Scott & Linton. Their premises were in the Woodyard at Dumbarton, Scotland, on the bank of the River Leven. William Scott was the business manager; Hercules Linton the designer. Linton had served his apprenticeship in Aberdeen with Alexander Hall & Sons, the inventors of the distinctive, hollow bow, and the most prolific builders of wooden clippers. He was also an experienced ship surveyor, particularly of iron ships.

But *Cutty Sark* was to be neither a wooden ship nor an iron ship, but one of composite construction. This consisted of a wrought-iron framework onto which wooden planks were bolted. It resulted in a very strong vessel but also one in which the frame took up a very small area of the hull, compared to the massive beams a wooden ship needed. This left more precious space for cargo. During the 1860s composite construction overtook wooden construction as the principal method of building sailing ships for the China trade. In 1869, thirteen composite ships (including *Cutty Sark*) were built for the trade and not one of wood. More composite ships were built in the yards around the Clyde than anywhere else in the country.

Today, apart from *Cutty Sark*, there are only two surviving composite vessels – the passenger clipper *City of Adelaide* and the sloop HMS *Gannet*.

Hercules Linton (1837-1900), designer of *Cutty Sark*.

Linton's drawing of *Cutty Sark*'s (half) midship section, showing the elements of her composite construction.

Right: John Willis (1817-1899), owner of *Cutty Sark*.

Cutty Sark, by Frederick Tudgay, 1872. This picture was commissioned by the ship's owner, John Willis.

BUILDING CUTTY SARK

S cott & Linton signed the agreement to build *Cutty Sark* on 28th January 1869.
Willis was to pay £16,150 and the ship was to be finished by the end
of July that year.

She was to have 138 iron frames, and a beam every fourth frame. A criss-cross
pattern of metal tie-plates along both sides, under the main and 'tween decks,
gave her the rigidity of an iron bridge. On each side, she has 36 strakes - runs
of planking from stem to stern, varying in thickness from six inches at the keel
to four inches at the top. The upper strakes were of teak from the west coast of
India, the lower ones rock elm from North America, better suited than teak to
constant immersion. More than 20,000 bolts secure the planks to the frames.

The hull was sheathed up to the waterline with thin plates of Muntz metal (a brass-like metal consisting of 60% copper and 40% zinc with just a trace of iron). This stopped weeds and barnacles from attaching themselves to the hull and kept out shipworm, but at a fraction of the cost of using copper, the traditional solution.

However, delays in design led to problems with Scott & Linton's cash-flow. The July deadline was missed. In the first week of September work in the yard was partially suspended. Scott & Linton's creditors then took over the ship and completed it.

Cutty Sark was launched with seemingly little fanfare on 22nd November 1869, then towed to the Leven shipyard for masting and on to Greenock on 20th December for the rigging that controlled the yards to be set up. She left Scotland on 13th January 1870. Just two weeks later she was taking on her first cargo in London's East India Docks.

Below: Cutty Sark on the stocks - a sketch by Hercules Linton, 1869.

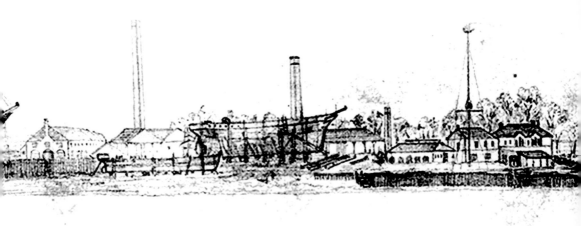

WHAT IS A 'CUTTY SARK'?

Almost all Willis's ships were named after rivers or villages in the area of the Scottish Borders that he came from – such as *The Tweed, Whiteadder* and *St. Abbs.* But the name 'cutty sark' is more obscure. It comes from Robert Burns' narrative poem *Tam O'Shanter*, published in 1791. The poem tells of how Tam gets drunk every market day in Ayr and what happens one such occasion when, in the evening, he rides his faithful horse Maggie home.

Tam rides the few miles to Alloway but is suddenly surprised to see lights in the church. Curious, he urges Maggie forward for a closer look. Peering through a window he sees that the church altar has been desecrated and the building is full of warlocks and witches dancing to a tune played on the bagpipes by the Devil himself.

Hercules Linton's design for the ship's figurehead.

The witches are all repulsive old hags, except one Nannie, a young beauty cavorting in a 'cutty sark' – a short shift.
ae winsome wench and waulie
Her cutty sark, o' Paisley harn,
That while a lassie she had worn,
In longitude tho' sorely scanty,
It was her best, and she was vauntie

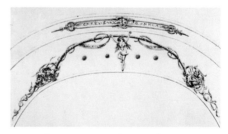

Hercules Linton's design for the stern decoration, with Tam O'Shanter on Nannie and the Devil on the bagpipes.

Tam, overwhelmed by the sight of Nannie in her revealing outfit cannot help but cry out...

Weel done, Cutty-sark!

The witches and warlocks now spot Tam and a wild chase begins. Tam urges Maggie to race for the Alloway bridge because he knows witches cannot cross water. Just as they reach the keystone of the bridge, Nannie grabs Maggie's tail, but horse and rider press on and escape, leaving Maggie's tail in Nannie's hand.

It is not surprising that Scotsman John Willis should take a name for his ship from the writings of his country's greatest poet. But why he chose to name the vessel after the undergarment of a witch, a creature unable to cross running water, remains a mystery.

The ship's figurehead is Nannie, dressed in a 'cutty sark' with her arm outstretched. One of the duties of the ship's apprentices, whenever she was in port, was to place a wad of unpicked rope in her hand to represent poor Maggie's tail.

The mast head vane – *Cutty Sark*'s emblem. It was thought lost after the ship lost her main mast in 1916 but turned up in a London auction house in 1960.

Tam O'Shanter
persued by Nannie.

CUTTY SARK'S
TEA VOYAGES 1870-1877

On 15th February 1870, *Cutty Sark* left London with a general cargo bound for Shanghai. Eight months later she returned with more than 600,000 kg of Chinese tea on board (enough to make more than 200 million cups). Even today, when tea is more commonly available, a cargo of this size would be worth more than £1 million. The records which would tell us exactly what types of tea these were have been destroyed, but by the mid-nineteenth century the British were greater consumers of black tea than green. 'Congou' was the generic name for good quality black tea but *Cutty Sark* may also have carried Lapsang Souchong, Bohea and Orange Pekoe. Popular green teas of the time were Gunpowder, Hyson and the now-forgotten Twankay.

The ship took 110 days to return to London from Shanghai. This was not outstanding and in fact she was never to match the times of the fastest tea clippers like *Thermopylae*, an Aberdeen-built composite clipper launched the year before *Cutty Sark* . However, only once did these two ships leave a Chinese port at the same time, so it is only this voyage that can be truly compared. Leaving Shanghai within minutes of each other on 17th June 1872, they kept pace until they reached the Indian Ocean. Picking up the brisk South-East trade winds, *Cutty Sark* raced ahead and by the time she was off the coast of South Africa, she was 400 miles ahead.

But then *Cutty Sark* ran into a heavy sea, and her rudder came away. Amazingly, on a ship that could no longer be steered, the carpenter managed to fashion a new temporary (or jury) rudder. A makeshift forge was built on the main deck to hammer out the new rudder's ironwork. At one point the forge overturned, showering the crew with hot coals.

The great tea port of Hankou.

After five days, they succeeded in hanging the rudder, including securing the lowest fixing, which was fifteen feet below the water. But by this time *Thermopylae* was 500 miles ahead. *Cutty Sark* lost even more time in the South Atlantic making running repairs to the jury rudder. *Thermopylae* reached London after 115 days at sea; *Cutty Sark* came in nine days later. However, it was the demonstration of seamanship by *Cutty Sark*'s captain and crew, rather than *Thermopylae*'s victory, that would be remembered.

Left: The jury rudder was lashed up during the 1872 passage from Shanghai to London. The figure at the stern is the ship's carpenter, Henry Henderson.

Cutty Sark in a Chinese Harbour, by Gerhard Geidel, 1991.

The end of the tea trade for sailing ships

I n 1870, *Cutty Sark* was one of 59 British sailing ships loading tea in China. In 1877, she was one of just nine. More and more tea was being loaded onto steamships rather than sailing ships.

From the early 1860s, steamships had competed with the clippers for tea cargoes but, possibly because so much of their hull space was devoted to coal bunkers, the sailing-ship owners did not view them as a serious threat to the trade. But as the steamers' engines became more efficient they began to make voyages as fast as the sailing clippers.

And then on 17th November 1869 (five days before *Cutty Sark* was launched), the Suez Canal was opened. This extraordinary feat of engineering, linking the Mediterranean with the Red Sea, cut 3,300 miles off the journey from China to London and ten to twelve days off the voyage… for a steamship. Unfortunately, the prevailing winds in the Red Sea are from the north-west, and the complicated wind patterns of the Mediterranean made it impractical for sailing ships to make use of the Canal. Now steamers, carrying almost twice as much tea as a sailing clipper, could reach London in 77 days.

In May 1878, *Cutty Sark* returned to Hankou but her captain was able to find only enough tea to fill half her hold. He took the ship back down the Yangtze to Shanghai, but again all the tea had been taken by the steamers. So he decided to take a coal cargo to Japan, in the hope that there would be tea available when he returned to Shanghai. But there was still none to be had. *Cutty Sark*'s days as a tea clipper were over. Instead she was forced to carry a variety of cargoes around the world, ending this voyage not in her home port of London but in New York.

Only once more in her career did she carry a tea cargo – this time Indian tea – from Calcutta to Melbourne in 1881. She would carry on 'tramping' – travelling from port to port with whatever cargoes could be found – until 1883.

The 'Hell-ship' voyage

T he crew on *Cutty Sark*, like those on most British clippers, seems to have been generally content with their officers. Most voyages passed without major incidents, certainly in comparison to some of the American clippers, dubbed the 'Hell-ships' because of their harsh masters and mates. But the voyage *Cutty Sark* began in 1880 was the exception – it was indeed a 'Hell-ship' voyage.

It started uneventfully with a passage from London to Penarth in Wales, to load coal for the American fleet at Yokohama. But on board were a tough and unpopular first mate, Sydney Smith, and a troublesome Chicago-born seaman called John Francis. After a number of confrontations, Francis rashly threatened Smith with one of the heavy wooden bars used to turn the capstan. Smith snatched the bar out of Francis's hand and struck him on the head with it. So hard was the blow that Francis died the following evening. Smith was confined to his cabin until the ship reached Anjer, a popular port of call on the western edge of Java. There, with the Captain's connivance, Smith escaped and left Anjer on board an American ship.

The incident was later the basis for the Joseph Conrad story, *The Secret Sharer*, although the mate in that story is a more sympathetic figure. The real-life Smith changed his name to John Anderson but two years later he was recognised in London, arrested, tried for murder and sentenced to seven years' hard labour for manslaughter.

Back on board *Cutty Sark*, the crew were outraged by their captain's complicity in Smith's escape and refused to work. Captain Wallace, who up until then had been a mild and popular master, was forced to put four of them in irons. This left the sailing of the ship to himself and the second mate, the sailmaker, the carpenter, the cook and four apprentices. But for three days the ship was becalmed, which gave Wallace plenty of time to consider his future. He must have realised that when they reached Yokohama he would at very least have his master's certificate suspended for helping Smith escape. In the early hours of the fourth day, 9th September 1880, Wallace spoke to the helmsman, stepped onto the rail at the stern of the ship and then stepped overboard. He was never seen again.

After returning to Anjer, a Dutch pilot took *Cutty Sark* to Singapore. There her coal cargo was being unloaded when the new captain appointed by Willis joined the ship. This was William Bruce, formerly the first mate of Willis's *Hallowe'en*.

Above:
Cutty Sark at sea, 1888, taken by Captain Woodget from one of the ship's boats.

He sailed her on to Calcutta where the crew were paid off, leaving only the apprentices and the carpenter. But *Cutty Sark* would be tied up in Calcutta for four months before a cargo could be found. She departed for Melbourne, then sailed on to Shanghai and Cebu in the Philippines before finally heading for the USA.

Bruce had not bothered to pick up sufficient provisions for the final leg of the voyage and found himself having to beg for food, first from a German ship and then from a Royal Navy ship. *Cutty Sark* finally docked in New York, 706 days after leaving London.

John Willis dismissed Bruce and transferred the entire crew of *Blackadder* to *Cutty Sark*. The ship set off once more on a 'tramp', to Semarang then on to the ports of India's east coast before returning to London in June 1883.

Carting wool bales to Sydney, c. 1880 – 1923.

THE WOOL VOYAGES 1883-95

In 1883, John Willis decided to put *Cutty Sark* into the trade of bringing Australian wool to London, one in which a number of former tea clippers, including *Thermopylae*, were already working. The Australian industry, specialising in Merino wool, had been expanding rapidly since its foundation in the early 1800s and by 1870 it was the world's largest producer of wool. Ships usually left Britain in the summer and returned with their bales of wool from Newcastle NSW, Sydney or Brisbane, for the London sales in the first few months of the new year.

On her very first voyage from Australia to London, *Cutty Sark* reached her home port in 84 days. It was the fastest passage made by any ship that year and she arrived 25 days or more ahead of the ships which had left about the same time. The following year, she did even better, returning in just 80 days. So pleased was John Willis that he rewarded the captain with the command of a larger vessel, the Willis flagship, *The Tweed*. *Cutty Sark*'s new captain, Richard Woodget, was even more successful. Again and again he brought the ship back to London in times that neither *Thermopylae* nor any other sailing vessel could match, the best being 73 days from Sydney to London.

In 1886, Willis - perhaps with the hope of setting a new sailing record – sent *Cutty Sark* out once more to Shanghai in the hope of a tea cargo. After three-and-a-half months searching in vain, Woodget abandoned the quest and headed to Sydney for wool.

However, not every voyage was as successful. The 1893 passage back to Europe was particularly hard, with the ship passing through icebergs on the way to Cape Horn and, as she approached the English Channel, two crewmen were washed off the bowsprit and lost.

Woodget not only improved on his predecessor's sailing times, he also managed to 'screw' more bales of wool into the hold. He usually supervised the loading himself but in 1894, possibly to teach him a lesson, the stevedores of Sydney took matters into their own hands and screwed in over 5,000 bales – considerably more than Woodget had managed.

Despite the speedy passages and the amount of wool the ship was carrying, John Willis had felt for some time that *Cutty Sark* was not making the money she once had: freight charges were dropping and his little ship was facing increasing competition for wool cargoes from larger vessels. Willis began to cut back on her upkeep and her gear was constantly being carried away in high seas. Finally, in 1895, three months after her return from Australia, he decided to sell her.

Above: Cutty Sark advert for wool.

Right: Cutty Sark at Circular Quay, Sydney, c. 1890

OTHER CARGOES

Although famous for transporting tea and wool, *Cutty Sark* carried other cargoes. She frequently carried coal in her hold and on her last four voyages as a tea clipper always sailed out via Sydney to pick up 1,000 tons of coal for Shanghai.

Tea and wool cargoes were light and would have made the ship unstable without significant ballast in the bottom of the hold. China could offer only stone ballast for the tea cargoes but when returning with wool *Cutty Sark* was ballasted with 200 tons of valuable chrome or nickel ore.

During her tramping period, the ship carried whatever cargo she could find. This might be scrap-iron destined for Shanghai, jute from the Philippines, deer horns and shark 'bones' from Australia or myrobolanes - a type of plum - from the Coromandel Coast of India.

Beer was also a common outward cargo, particularly for Australia. On her way down the Thames *Cutty Sark* would also often stop at Gravesend to pick up gunpowder from the Kent mills, destined for the Australian gold and coal mines.

Leaving London for China or Sydney, she always had a general cargo in her hold, made up of a very large number of small packages. In 1872, for example, she departed for Shanghai carrying baking powder, cocoa, currants, fruits, liquorice, marmalade, sugar, tobacco, brandy, sherry, wine, hops, malt seeds, drugs, mercury and other chemicals, oils and paints, galvanised iron, shot-iron, iron sheets, timber, tin plates, plated ware, earthenware and glassware, anvils, spades, nails, bolts, paper, books, machinery, engine springs, pianos and other musical instruments, boots and shoes, candles and matches.

Hong Kong harbour, looking west, c.1880. *Cutty Sark* called here in 1872, with a cargo of rice from Bangkok.

TO FOLLOW THE "WHITEADDER."

DIRECT FOR

SHANGHAI,

The magnificent New Clyde-built Clipper,

CUTTY-SARK, A I. 16 YEARS,

(Owned by Messrs. JOHN WILLIS & SON,)

900 Tons Register, G. MOODIE, Commander,
(Late of the "LAUDERDALE.")

Loading in the East India Docks.

This Vessel, just launched, is, from her fine lines, expected to prove one of the fastest afloat.

For Freight or Passage, apply to

GELLATLY, HANKEY, SEWELL & CO.,

8, York Street, MANCHESTER; and
109, Leadenhall Street, LONDON, E.C.

Above:
The Bund at
Shanghai,
c. 1880.
Cutty Sark
delivered a cargo
of coal here
several times.

Below:
Advertisement for
Cutty Sark.

Cutty Sark under sail

Length overall: 86 metres (280 feet)
Beam: 11 metres (36 feet)
Depth: 7 metres (22 feet 6 inches)
Max sail area: 3,000m² (32,000 square feet)
Net tonnage: 921 tons

Signal flags: JKWS, code for
the ship's owner Jock Willis

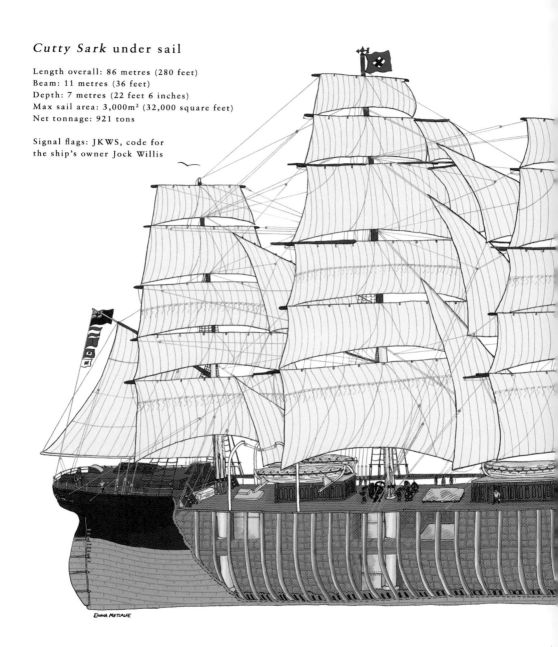

EMMA METCALFE

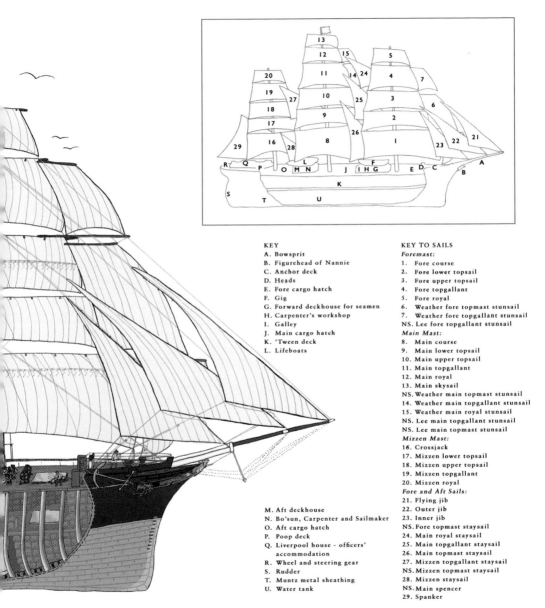

KEY
A. Bowsprit
B. Figurehead of Nannie
C. Anchor deck
D. Heads
E. Fore cargo hatch
F. Gig
G. Forward deckhouse for seamen
H. Carpenter's workshop
I. Galley
J. Main cargo hatch
K. 'Tween deck
L. Lifeboats

M. Aft deckhouse
N. Bo'sun, Carpenter and Sailmaker
O. Aft cargo hatch
P. Poop deck
Q. Liverpool house - officers'
   accommodation
R. Wheel and steering gear
S. Rudder
T. Muntz metal sheathing
U. Water tank

KEY TO SAILS
Foremast:
1.   Fore course
2.   Fore lower topsail
3.   Fore upper topsail
4.   Fore topgallant
5.   Fore royal
6.   Weather fore topmast stunsail
7.   Weather fore topgallant stunsail
NS. Lee fore topgallant stunsail
Main Mast:
8.   Main course
9.   Main lower topsail
10. Main upper topsail
11. Main topgallant
12. Main royal
13. Main skysail
NS. Weather main topmast stunsail
14. Weather main topgallant stunsail
15. Weather main royal stunsail
NS. Lee main topgallant stunsail
NS. Lee main topmast stunsail
Mizzen Mast:
16. Crossjack
17. Mizzen lower topsail
18. Mizzen upper topsail
19. Mizzen topgallant
20. Mizzen royal
Fore and Aft Sails:
21. Flying jib
22. Outer jib
23. Inner jib
NS. Fore topmast staysail
24. Main royal staysail
25. Main topgallant staysail
26. Main topmast staysail
27. Mizzen topgallant staysail
NS. Mizzen topmast staysail
28. Mizzen staysail
NS. Main spencer
29. Spanker

NS: Not shown

Based on the painting by Frederick Tudgay, 1872

Crewing Cutty Sark

When *Cutty Sark* left London in 1870 for her first China voyage, she had 27 men on board – seventeen able seamen, two ordinary seamen, a sailmaker, a carpenter and his mate, the first and second mate, a steward (to look after the officers), a cook and the master. This was a typical sized crew for her tea-clipper years. However, in 1880, her masts and yards were cut down in size (losing her skysail and the stunsails) so that fewer men would be needed to handle her. In 1890, for example, she left London with just nineteen men in total – of which nine were seamen and three were apprentices. Sailmakers, always on board on the early voyages, became less frequently engaged but there was always a carpenter.

Most of the seamen who sailed on *Cutty Sark* did so just once. They were engaged voyage by voyage, so as soon as they returned to London they were paid off and had to look for another ship. But many took the opportunity of a one-way passage to Australia. In 1876, for example, twelve of the sixteen able seamen deserted. They were replaced with Australian seamen, who were generally unpopular because they had to be paid substantially more than those who had signed on in London.

However, two men sailed on the ship on ten voyages – Captain Richard Woodget and James Robson, the cook. They both joined *Cutty Sark* at the same time and only left when Willis sold her.

The youngest of those on board were fourteen- year-old apprentices, the oldest fifty-four- year-old able seamen. Most were British but Americans, Scandinavians and West Indians also signed on. There was even one man from China – the cook James Robson. He had been found floating at sea in a basket as a baby off the coast of China, rescued and brought up in England.

The names of 658 men are listed as having sailed on *Cutty Sark* during her 25 voyages under the British flag. She sailed in the world's most dangerous seas and often in storms, and yet in 25 years only five men were lost overboard.

Robert Kemp, First Mate, 1893-94.

Captain Woodget (back row, wearing a Tam O'Shanter), his crew and guests on board, 1887, in Sydney.

Tony Robson, the cook (right) with Third Mate James Weston (left) c. 1888. Photograph by Captain Woodget.

Repairing a sail on *Cutty Sark's* poop deck, watched by the ship's boy. Photograph by Captain Woodget.

THE MASTERS ⚭

D uring her career under British colours, seven masters served on board
Cutty Sark. The first was Scotsman George Moodie who had overseen the
building of the ship and was captain for her first three voyages. However, when
the rudder was lost in the famous 1872 race with the *Thermopylae*, he had such
a furious argument with John Willis's brother Robert, who was on board and
tried to force Moodie to head for the nearest port, that he resigned as soon as
they reached London and went off to work on the steamers.

His replacement was Francis Moore, the shore superintendent for the Willis fleet.
A Yorkshireman then aged 50 and effectively retired, he agreed to command
Cutty Sark for a single voyage. The captaincy then passed to William Edward
Tiptaft. A Scotsman from the same area of Scotland as the Willis family, he was
a cautious but successful sailor. However, in 1878, on his sixth voyage, he fell ill
in Shanghai and died, aged just 35. James Smith Wallace from Aberdeen, the first
mate, took over and proved to be a popular captain, an excellent seaman and a
good driver of the ship. Unfortunately, his time coincided with the period when
it was becoming increasingly difficult to secure tea cargoes. His third voyage
– the 'Hell-ship' voyage during which Able Seaman Francis was killed – ended
in his suicide in the South China Sea.

The next captain, William Bruce, was a
heavy drinker, an unpopular commander
and a poor captain. An attempt to blame
the second mate for all the ship's troubles
during the 'Hell-ship' voyage backfired,
and cost Bruce his certificate.

Bruce was replaced by Captain Moore of
Blackadder (no relation to Francis Moore,
the second captain). It was he who first filled
Cutty Sark's hold with Australian wool and
immediately established her as the fastest of
all the sailing ships in the wool trade.

Captain Woodget's dogs.

Photographed Jany 13th 1888 by Captain Woodget. Cutty Sark . 290 ft high
400 West of Cape Horn. Lat 62°38' S. Long 140°30' W.

Capt Moodie in a storm

If Moore was a great captain, his replacement was a brilliant one. Norfolk-born Richard Woodget sailed the ship harder, established more records and squeezed more wool into her hull. He also found time to breed prize-winning collies (which were confined to the poop deck) and to learn to ride a bicycle on the 'tween deck. Thanks to one of the apprentices, son of the famous portrait photographer J.J.E. Mayall, Woodget became a keen photographer himself and left a unique record of the ship and the iceberg-laden seas through which she sailed.

Above:
Icebergs encountered on the way to Cape Horn - photograph by Captain Woodget.

Below:
Captain Moodie, catching forty winks.

THE END OF THE CLIPPER ERA

B y 1895, only ten of the graceful clippers that had worked in the China trade were still afloat. The rest had been wrecked, foundered or condemned. They were not replaced – the next generation of ocean-going sailing ships were four-masted steel barques with much larger carrying capacities and much less elegant. The sailing barques would continue in the Australian grain trade until the middle of the 20th century, but the fast clipper-ship days were over. *Cutty Sark*'s great rival, *Thermopylae*, left the wool trade in 1890 and, after a period in the Pacific, was acquired by the Portuguese navy and sailed in to Lisbon in 1897. In 1907 they used her for target practice and she now lies sunk at the mouth of the River Tagus. The only remnant of the tea clippers, apart from *Cutty Sark*, is the beached skeleton of *Ambassador*, once a composite ship like *Cutty Sark* but now stripped of her planking and lying at Estancia San Gregorio in Chile. She had been towed there from the Falkland Islands after a failed attempt to round Cape Horn in 1895.

This was the same year that *Cutty Sark* was sold. John Willis, who would live for only another four years, had already disposed of most of his fleet and on 6th July 1895, *Cutty Sark* was bought by a mercantile clerk, John Richards. He owned her for just sixteen days before selling her for £1,250 to the Lisbon-based company, Joaquim Antunes Ferreira & Cº, who re-named her *Ferreira*.

The Suez Canal - a shortcut for steamships.

Right: The steamship *Louden Castle* unloading tea in the London Docks, 1877.

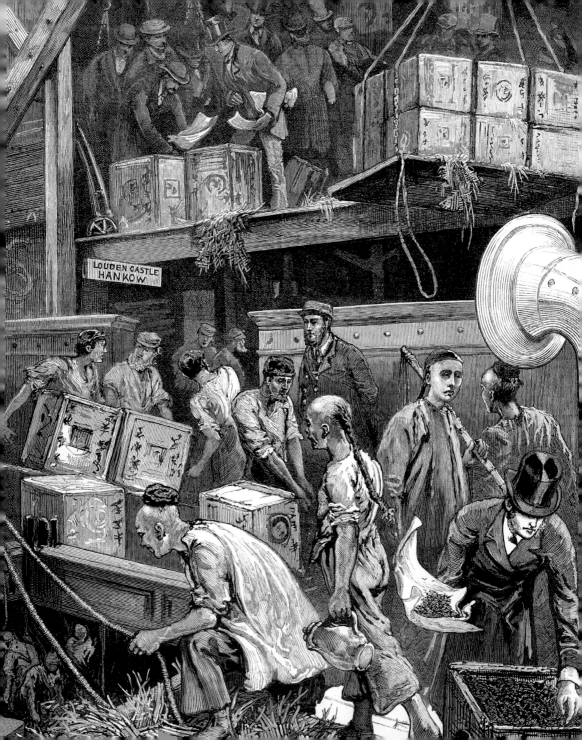

LOUDEN CASTLE
HANKOW

UNDER THE PORTUGUESE FLAG

Before the First World War, *Ferreira* transported cargoes around the world in a vast triangle, sailing from Lisbon to Portugal's African colonies, then on to Brazil, Barbados or the southern ports of the United States before returning to Lisbon. She was in Pensacola, Florida, when the Great Hurricane of 1906 struck. Considering that 5,000 homes were damaged and 134 people died, the ship was lucky to survive, although it was six months before she was seaworthy again.

She had an even luckier escape in May 1916. Sailing from Delagoa Bay in Mozambique to Mossamedes in Angola, she ran into a storm and her coal cargo began to shift to one side, making her dangerously unstable and difficult to sail. For nine days the storm raged. In order to save the ship, the captain had no choice but to order more and more of the masts and rigging to be cut away, until only the foremast and fore topmast remained. Finally a passing steamer managed to attach a line and tow *Ferreira* into South Africa's Table Bay.

Ferreira after the storm in 1916 with only her lower foremast remaining.

Partly because of cost and partly because of the wartime shortage of timber, *Ferreira* was re-rigged not as a ship but as a barquentine – a vessel with square sails on the foremast but triangular fore-and-aft sails on the main and mizzen masts. This needed a smaller crew but meant less canvas was spread, and so much of her speed was lost.

It was not until January 1918, twenty months after the storm, that *Ferreira* was fully repaired and ready to go to sea again. She was sold later that year to another Portuguese ship-owner, João Pires Correia, and she became an infrequent visitor to Britain. In 1922, after calling at London, she put into Falmouth with minor damage, and stayed for two months. In June that same year, she was sold again to Cia de Navegaçao de Portugal, Lisbon, who named her *Maria do Amparo* ('Mary that shelters', a reference to the Virgin Mary).

Ferreira at Pensacola, Florida, 1906.

Right: Ferreira in Limehouse, London, 1921.

SAVED FOR THE NATION

When *Ferreira* called into Falmouth in 1922, she was spotted by a retired sea captain called Wilfred Dowman. Despite her battered and much-altered appearance, he recognised her as *Cutty Sark*, the same vessel which had surged past him in 1895 when he was a sixteen-year-old apprentice on board the sailing ship *Hawkdale*. He was determined to save her for the nation and pursued her back to Portugal.

It was Dowman's vision which saved *Cutty Sark*, but credit also belongs to his wife Catharine. She was a member of the wealthy Courtauld family, famous for its textile manufacturing, and so had far more resources than her retired sea-captain husband. These enabled them to buy the ship – now renamed *Maria do Amparo* – for £3,750, very much more than her commercial value, and considerably more than the price she had been sold for twenty-seven years earlier.

Between 1922 and 1938, *Cutty Sark* left Falmouth only once- in 1924, to be the flagship at the Fowey Regatta.

She was towed all the way from Portugal, reaching Falmouth on 2nd October 1922. Re-registered as *Cutty Sark*, she was moored off the foreshore of Trefussis Fields, Flushing, in Falmouth Harbour, and Dowman set about restoring her to clipper-ship appearance.

Dowman wanted *Cutty Sark* primarily as a sail-training ship, to train boys in the skills of seamanship. Cadets lived on board during the summer months. However, he also opened her as an attraction, with visitors arriving by rowing boat. This began shortly before the public could go on board HMS *Victory*, so *Cutty Sark* was the first historic ship to be open as an attraction since Sir Francis Drake's *Golden Hind* at Deptford in the 1580s.

Cutty Sark in Falmouth, restored as a clipper ship.

It was not only seamanship skills that were taught to the cadets on board.

BACK TO THE THAMES ✑

Wilfred Dowman died in 1936, just after his fifty-seventh birthday, leaving no-one to take over the ship in Falmouth. Fortunately, the Incorporated Thames Nautical College at Greenhithe, on the River Thames, offered her a berth and Mrs Dowman presented the ship to them – along with a gift of £5,000 for her upkeep. In 1938 *Cutty Sark* made her last sea voyage, under tow, to her new home, alongside the *Worcester*, an old 86-gun warship. *Cutty Sark* was a welcome addition to the establishment – and a much more practical vessel for teaching sail-drill than *Worcester*.

The outbreak of the Second World War saw *Cutty Sark*'s topmasts and topgallant masts lowered and her upper yards struck, to reduce her size as a target from enemy bombers. She was also converted to an emergency shelter for the College's cadets if there was a gas or bomb attack. Her decks were made gas-proof, sandbags were filled with ballast from her hold, decontamination showers were installed, and boarding nets and ladders were placed over her sides for fast embarking and disembarking.

In the event, these preparations proved unnecessary. The Government decided to evacuate all training ships and the College moved to Foots Cray Place in south-east London. Ironically, their new site suffered substantial bomb damage while *Cutty Sark* survived the war unscathed.

However, little regular maintenance was undertaken during those years, and by the end of the war she was in desperate need of a refit. But the College's priorities now lay elsewhere. In January 1946, they had taken possession of a new *Worcester* from the Admiralty – the former HMS *Exmouth* – and the College's resources were now ploughed into converting her into a modern training vessel. Neither sail training nor *Cutty Sark* was wanted.

Right: Cadets on the ship at Greenhithe.

TO GREENWICH

I t was now that Frank Carr, the Director of the National Maritime Museum, stepped forward as the third saviour of *Cutty Sark*. He persuaded the London County Council to make the site of the badly bomb-damaged Ship Hotel in Greenwich available for *Cutty Sark*. He even persuaded them to pay for the ship to be towed to Millwall Docks in February 1951 for a survey and a coat of paint, before she was anchored off Deptford as part of the Festival of Britain. She stayed there until October as a test of public reaction to her possible permanent preservation.

Crucially, Carr had also engaged the support and enthusiasm of HRH The Duke of Edinburgh. This led to the establishment of the Cutty Sark Preservation Society, which succeeded in raising the £250,000 needed for the restoration from members of the public.

On 10th December 1954, *Cutty Sark* was floated into her purpose-built dock on a high tide, with less than half a metre between the keel and the concrete bottom. When the tide retreated, the dock emptied and the channel linking it to the River Thames was filled up.

The ship had been altered during her years under the Portuguese flag, and at Falmouth and Greenhithe. A decision was made to restore the ship to her appearance around 1872, after the forward deckhouse had been installed. This was achieved after a great deal of research and a few minor compromises (for example, the Portuguese access to the officers' accommodation was retained, to ease visitor flow).

Part of the justification for saving *Cutty Sark* was the wish to preserve her as a permanent memorial to the Merchant Navy, and particularly those lost in the two world wars.

Cutty Sark, East India Dock 13 September 1954, showing restoration of the deck, by James McBey, who also designed the Cutty Sark whisky label.

The sculptor Maurice Lambert (1901 – 64) was commissioned to design a memorial wreath. Its accompanying plaques read:

IN MEMORY OF THOSE WHOSE SERVICE IN THE MERCHANT NAVY HELPED TO ENLARGE THE LIVELIHOOD OF BRITAIN AND PROTECT THE FREEDOM OF THE BRITISH COMMONWEALTH OF NATIONS.

HERE TO COMMEMORATE AN ERA THE CUTTY SARK HAS BEEN PRESERVED AS A TRIBUTE TO THE SHIPS AND MEN OF THE MERCHANT NAVY IN THE DAYS OF SAIL.

The second plaque ends with the couplet: *They mark our passage as a race of men. Earth will not see such ships as these again.* These are the final lines in John Masefield's poem *Ships*, published in 1912. Masefield was also the Poet Laureate at this time.

Above:
Cutty Sark entering her Greenwich dock, 1954.

Cutty Sark was opened to the public by HM Queen Elizabeth II on 25th June 1957.

Conserving the Cutty Sark by John Bryce.

THE 2006-2012 CONSERVATION PROJECT

B etween 1957 and 2003 more than thirteen million visitors walked the decks of *Cutty Sark*, making her one of London's most successful tourist attractions. However, the belief that the 1950s' restoration would preserve the ship forever soon proved over-optimistic. The sheathing had to be replaced in the 1960s and by the 1970s the iron framework began to show signs of weakness. A survey completed in the mid-1990s concluded that the ship would collapse within the next decade unless major efforts were made to stop the deterioration of the iron and put some strength back into her hull. It was estimated that more than 60 per cent of fastenings holding the planking to the iron framework had failed. In addition, the deck, which had been repeatedly repaired over the years, continued to leak badly. Worst of all, the support system of props and shores was beginning visibly to distort the ship's shape – her most significant attribute. *Cutty Sark* was clearly in need of major conservation if she was to survive.

Recognising her importance to the nation's maritime history, the Heritage Lottery Fund and a number of other supporters stepped forward as the next saviours, funding the plans to replace the leaking deck, take off all the planks to treat the ironwork, and introduce a new support system. The aim was not to restore the ship to the appearance of being seaworthy, but to conserve her – that is, to ensure the long-term stability of as much of the ship's fabric from her working life (1869-1922) as possible. Because of her composite construction of iron and wood – each requiring very different treatments – it would be one of the most complex conservation projects ever undertaken on a historic ship.

In November 2006, the ship closed to the public and work began. Then, in the early hours of Monday 21st May 2007, a serious fire broke out. The London Fire Brigade (the fifth saviour) very quickly brought the blaze under control. By great good fortune, a very large number of the hull planks had been removed for conservation. Some of the metal framework was distorted but not more than five per cent of the ship's original fabric was lost.

The fire delayed the project considerably, but work continued and in spring 2011 one of the most important elements of the scheme took place: to relieve the keel of the weight of the ship, to preserve her unique shape – and to allow visitors to see her beautiful form properly – *Cutty Sark* was raised over three metres into the air.

Finally, *Cutty Sark* was re-opened by Her Majesty The Queen on 25th April 2012, almost 55 years after she had first performed this task.

April 2008: the ship's counter is removed for conservation.

April 2008: members of the conservation team working on the stern of the ship after the removal of the counter.

Cutty Sark lifted
Tim Keeler.

Enduring fame

Cutty Sark was already a celebrated ship when she was making her record-breaking runs back from Australia. During her long-enforced stay in Cape Town, under the Portuguese flag, her crew were happy to show this legendary clipper to curious visitors who knew of her. There were even attempts to save her for the nation years before Captain Dowman was successful.

In March 1923, London wine merchants Berry Brothers & Rudd, invited James McBey, one of Scotland's famous artists, to lunch. The conversation turned to the company's plan to create their own blend of whisky for export to the American market – as soon as Prohibition ended (although this would not, in fact, be for another ten years). But what to call the whisky? *Cutty Sark*'s recent return to Britain had been headline news and so 'Cutty Sark' was proposed as a memorable name. McBey sketched out a design for the label there and then - the clipper in full sail - and one of the world's most famous brands was born.

Cutty Sark was also an inspiration to circumnavigator (Sir) Francis Chichester, who in 1967 recreated the Australian run of the wool clippers in his ketch *Gipsy Moth IV*. Similarly, it was a boyhood visit to the ship that inspired Stephen Paine to take up naval architecture as a career: he went on to design *Queen Mary II*. She has also been – and continues to be – an inspiration to countless thousands of others: no other ship has ever been so frequently modelled and painted.

When *Cutty Sark* caught fire in 2007, enquiries about the extent of the damage flooded in from all corners of the globe, even from countries with no obvious associations with the ship. This was a clear demonstration that *Cutty Sark* remains one of the most famous and best loved ships in the world, alongside USS *Constitution* and HMS *Victory*.

This beautiful ship is the epitome of an era, the last authentic reminder of the great days of sail.

Bust of Sir Francis Chichester (1901-72).

Right: One of a number of pictures of the ship painted by John Everett in the 1920s and 1930s.

THE FIGUREHEAD COLLECTION ⤫

Cutty Sark's own figurehead of Nannie is no longer the beautiful witch the designer Hercules Linton envisaged. Dangerous seas took away her original head and an arm.

Nannie is displayed in the Sammy Ofer Gallery amid the largest collection of figureheads in the world. All of them are from merchant ships and all, with the exception of Nannie, are part of the Long John Silver Collection. 'Long John Silver' was Sydney Cumbers (1875–1959). An accident with a toy gun as a child cost him the sight of his left eye, which resulted in a distinctive eye-patch. Later in life it gave him the nickname Long John or Captain Silver. He was a successful businessman but one with a passion for maritime artefacts, building up a collection of 101 figureheads, as well as a host of models and maritime paraphernalia. This collection was displayed in Gravesend in The Look-Out, on the seafront, belonging to the Clarendon Hotel. The expiry of the lease on The Look-Out coincided with the restoration of *Cutty Sark*, and in 1953 Captain Silver donated the collection to the ship.

Part of the collection resembles an exhibition, in wood, of the great and good of Victorian Britain, with representations of such figures as Disraeli, Gladstone, General Gordon and Florence Nightingale. Many of the figureheads came from ships which have never been identified, and were probably salvaged from wrecks.

Captain Silver dedicated his collection to the Little Ships of Dunkirk, but the figureheads' varied and sometimes veiled history makes them a fitting memorial to all those who have served in the merchant service.

Figurehead from *Gladstone*

Figurehead from an unknown ship

Figurehead from
Rising Sun

ACKNOWLEDGEMENTS

Written by Dr Eric Kentley, based primarily on the books by David MacGregor, Basil Lubbock, articles by Alan Platt and Simon Waite and research undertaken by Cutty Sark Trust curators Jessica Lewis and Simon Schofield. The text was edited by Dr Pieter van der Merwe.

Designed by Paul Collins, Perception Design.
Project managed by Nathan Saker.
Printed by Belmont Press.

The Cutty Sark Trust gratefully acknowledges the use of images from the following copyright holders:
Mr & Mrs Brettle: p. 22; p. 24 (top and bottom)
J. Bryce: p. 56
Felix Rosenstiel's Widow & Son Ltd: cover
Guardian Newspapers: p.58 (bottom)
HSBC: p. 38, p. 39 (top)
T. Keeler: p. 59
E. Kentley: p. 28 (top and bottom); p. 46
Emma Metcalfe: pp. 40-41.
Museum Of London: p.47
National Maritime Museum (Royal Museums Greenwich): p.12; pp.16-17; p. 43 (bottom left and bottom right); p. 45 (bottom); p. 48; p. 49; p. 50; p.53; p. 61
National Portrait Gallery, London: p. 11
Peabody Essex Museum: p.8
Powerhouse Museum, Sydney: p. 34
Smithsonian Institution, NMAH/Transportation: p.48 (bottom)
State Library of Victoria, NSW: p. 33; p.50
Copyright of all other images is held by The Cutty Sark Trust

Principal sponsor:

Printed on Essential Silk, an FSC-certified stock sourced from fully sustainable forests, using vegetable based inks